MW00915146

EATING

DISORDERS

A SIMPLE GUIDE TO OVERCOMING

BINGE EATING

BY

JASON B. TILLER

ACKNOWLEDGEMENTS

This book could not have been written without the guidance and generosity of many people. To all of you who encouraged and stood by me, thank you.

Copyright © 2017 Jason B. Tiller

DISCALIMER

This guide is not a replacement to competent medical advice from appropriate health care professionals and the information contained therein should not be taken as the holy grail for any reason. It is intended to provide information to aid people having a hard time with eating disorders, especially "Binge Eating". This guide was written from a wealth of experience observing and helping out close family members and friends who have struggled with and managed eating disorders.

Table of Contents

"Cookies are made of butter and love." ~

Norwegian Proverb

FREE DOWNLOAD

A Mouthful of Glory

Get your free copy of "A Mouthful of Glory". It is a guide for athletes, coaches and loved ones on how to navigate the difficult terrain of eating disorders. Go to the website below to get your copy.

http://wp.me/P9gR5N-u

INTRODUCTION

Persons with eating disorders do not eat food for its nutritional qualities. Rather it is used as a coping mechanism for some underlying emotional troubles. This is referred to as emotional eating and it acts as a mood enhancer and comfort crouch. A lot of persons find solace in food to manage emotional trauma to feel some level of relief. Eating may be used as a means to get the mind off such feelings and it may be restrictive or excessive. When an individual becomes hooked to this method of coping with emotional troubles without having control, it becomes a rather ugly issue. Walking away from this habit can be hard and the road to recovery must involve treatment of both the mental and physical sides of the condition. Paying attention only to the nutritional or psychological aspect alone is a battle half won.

The internalized views of a self-esteem that has been battered is one component of binge eating disorder and most other eating conditions. Fixing the body and the mind is very important and lies at the center of the whole process. Also, important are triggering factors all around us and taking pre-emptive steps on how to minimize them.

Having the ability to make choices to determine what you want when you want it and not been compelled by your feelings of self-doubt is a pointer to walking down the path to recovery. Getting healthier varies for all individuals. Some can do it all alone with the power of their will while others will need help from family, friends and medical professionals.

CHAPTER ONE

WHAT IS BINGE EATING?

We all tend to feed to stupor from time to time mostly during festive periods or during celebrations and we are aware that we have taken in more than we should. Certain individuals who overeat feel a sense of guilt and despair at this act. The reason been that they try to control the challenges they are facing in their lives by bingeing on food. The pull to feed on large amounts of food is almost irresistible. This actions or habit which forms a dependent base for such individuals is called Binge Eating Disorder (BED). Bulimia Nervosa is another eating disorder similar to binge eating. However, the only difference is that in bulimia, the food taken in is immediately expelled from the body through vomiting, use of laxatives etc. As with other eating disorders, the urge to think less about food only makes it harder leading to episodes of restricting nutrient intakes for long periods of time or overeating.

The American Psychiatric Association (APA) defined Binge Eating Disorder as recurring episodes of eating significantly more food in a short period of time than most people would eat under similar circumstances, with episodes marked by feelings of lack of control. Patients eat rather fast even in situations when hunger is not in the picture. The individual often experiences feelings of shame and lack of worth and bingeing is the way out to hide this habits. It occurs regularly at least once a week for a period of three months.

CAUSES OF BINGE EATING DISORDER

Several factors coming together in various proportions can lead to the development of the disorder and the level of seriousness and causative factors differ from one person to the other. Family pressures, mental and physical issues, environmental influences are some of the major determinants of the disorder. Your psychological makeup can make you predisposed to having a binge eating disorder. Feelings of the inability to deal with everyday life situations, depression, low self-worth are a few of the psychological factors that can precede the disorder. They are most times associated with negative life experiences and having a hard time dealing with such makes a person turn to the easiest alternative which is food.

Most persons dealing with an eating disorder tend to go to the extreme in dealing with life issues and see the world in black and white with no grey in between. They set the bars high in their emotional, professional, relationships and other spheres of their lives. They berate themselves when they fall short of set targets which are often very hard to attain. The environment plays a major role in the development of an eating disorder with the media subtly pushing the message of ultra-thinness into our subconscious. These body types are associated with a level of prestige, success, wealth that the general population is mostly lacking. We are controlled into believing that the without us having such body types, we lack self-control and the will power to be successful and belong to the elite class. In families and other settings where persons who are in a position of authority have problems with body images will often pass on the message to those looking up to them.

Some factors that predispose one to a binge eating disorder includes; trying to have an absolutely perfect life, negative body image, an unstable family life, societal values of human body size and shape, physical or sexual abuse, traumatic event in the life of the individual like the loss of a loved one etc.

The standout precipitating indices of binge eating disorder is dieting brought about by physical and mental variables. When we are hungry, it is only natural to eat. However, when we become obsessed with our diet and all things relating to food, we are likely to be thrown off the bull and gored badly. Such an individual goes on an eating spree if a break is had from the tightly controlled dieting program he or she is on.

The social factor involves our interactions with other individuals in our community and the family. Comments and actions of bullying about your body can bring about the disorder. Feeling the pressure to fit in or get along with your friends who are on some sort of dieting or new eating fad can set off the habit.

Getting a hold of the causative factor of your bingeing disorder can be a herculean task which is very important if your wholesome journey to recovery is to begin in earnest. Understanding the factors will become more obvious to you once you have made an effort to get control over your eating habits. Once they come to the fore, it will be easier for you to deal with them effectively. You have to know that making your own choices is what recovery is all about. Asking for help from loved ones and professionals does not indicate that you are not making your own choices, it is just a way for you to get support and guidance while you create your own path to a healthier life.

EFFECTS AND HEALTH CONSEQUENCES

Just like with any deviation from normal health, there are bound to be consequences that you will have to bear. It ranges from the mild to very serious life threatening effects. For you as a person battling with binge eating, obesity is one result. An obese person will suffer from a deposition of fatty material in the blood vessels leading to strokes, weakening of the vessels etc., diabetes, high blood pressure and a host of other conditions. Ladies will most likely experience irregular menstrual circles, insomnia, poor digestion etc.

Mentally, feelings of shame and depressive tendencies are quite common. Obsessive

Compulsive Disorder around food is quite common and a fear of people assisting you during this trying times.

Most eating disorders are easily recognized by some indicators and they experience some of the symptoms and behavioral patterns associated with that eating disorder. Patients suffering from binge eating often prefer to eat in secret away from the eyes of the general public while putting up a façade of normalcy in front of loved ones. A point to be noted is that when an individual feel that he or she has binged, it is not always to be assumed that massive amount of food had been consumed. The bingeing process differs with every individual as it may simply refer to when one eats what wasn't planned for, or simply feeling compelled to eat. The emotional troubles a person is facing may open a pathway to bingeing as a way for handling such problems. Food consumed by this class of people are what others will shy away due to the high fat and calorie content. The food is usually gulped down without proper mastication and enjoyment which ought to be one of the pleasures of eating. While this process is going on, the individual is already thinking of the next meal. The intake of such large amounts of carbs and fat may lead to the individual becoming obese but that is not always the situation as some appear normal.

The trap of binge eating involves one getting caught in an unending cycle of engaging in some form of nutrient intake control, massive overeating, self-punishment and self-despise. The feeling of been alone is expressed in the tendency to always wanting to eat alone to mask the shame of the eating habit.

A binge expresses itself in several stages. The first is the building up of tension which is caused by a lot of underlying and mostly unknown factors. You may have a nagging sensation of something not just been right and despite your continuous mental search, it eludes you. Slowly and with all certainty, you can feel it getting closer building up the tension as it pushes you into a corner. To let off the steam from the tension for you to feel a sense of relief, you turn to food as source of distraction from the negative feelings. This stage acts as a "slate cleaner" which temporarily suppresses all the pent up tension. It however only lasts for a short while leaving you tired and experiencing what is called a hangover. The next stage is characterized by tiredness, body pains, vomiting. After all these, a commitment is made to put all the negative feelings and the bingeing process behind and never engage in them again. You make promises not to eat much the day or next or to go on a diet. It is most times a short lived victory.

CHAPTER TWO

TREATMENT AND SUPPORT

At some point you will have to get external help to assist you moving out of the clutches of the disorder. It is not just going to leave you on its accord, an effort on your part is needed. You may get rid of it based on the strength of your self will while others will require the support of loved ones and medical professionals. Getting out of your relative safe environment with total control over your emotions by bingeing will be having your whole existence threatened and you will do everything you can to resist the attempt to help you out. Within you, your inner voice is telling you this is not right and that you are hurting yourself and those around you. You have to make contact with the outside world if truly you want to make recovery and move away from such harmful habits. This is a time when your willpower has to be really strong to totally subdue any doubts about you reaching out for help.

SELF HELP

Educating yourself about your condition is the first building block in the construction of an edifice to your good health. You will have to discover and make findings on different methods that are available to treating your condition. Basically, a number of self-help techniques coax your inner feelings that have been buried but having effects on you to the surface for you to have a look at them and know what is giving them strength. Once you are in this position, the likelihood is that you will have control over them and in essence your disorder. Helping yourself also includes following the advice of trained personnel and use of guides like this book you are reading to make informed decisions. You may decide to work with a group for your recovery process or professionals. No one way works the same way for two different individuals and it is very common to combine several methods for effective healing process. If you decide to go down the road of recovery all by yourself and in the process you find it too challenging, it is advisable you get assistance.

If you decide to battle the disorder all by yourself, some of the following information will be invaluable to your recovery process. Making an informed decision all boils down to studying what the self-help method is about. You may have employed other methods that may have worked or not for you in the past but going through this steps outlined, you will definitely find something new that you can incorporate into your own personal program.

SETTING UP A DIET REGIME

The singular paramount step to changing your eating habit is to eat regularly. Do not go for extended periods without having some form of food. At least eat something every 4 hours. Your body system needs regular supply of fuel for maximum functioning. So you yo-yoing between serious dietary restrictions and massive overloading of your system can bring your system to a grinding halt. Our bodies are designed in such a way that once there is a reduced calorie intake, bodily functions begin to slow down just like in hibernating animals during the winter resulting in decreased bodily functions. So when you constantly cut down on your nutrient consumptions, your organs will have reduced functions which is detrimental to your general well-being. So getting back on track with a proper eating habit and regular eating process is one and most of the important steps in getting better.

Constant and regular intake of calories is a perfect way to stop the vicious circle that your binge has got you trapped in. Embrace each new day and in setting up your meal plan, make sure you don't aim too high to prevent putting too much pressure on yourself. Starting small with plans that you can comfortably deal with will strengthen you considerably to eventually take on fairly tougher challenges in the not too distant future. Keeping record of times, you eat and when next you should take something in is an important step. After each meal or snack, you should have something again after the next three hours. Having a time frame of when next you are to eat keeps your mind at rest and put the anxiety and worries at bay and thus the propensity to binge is almost certainly put away. It is a battle of wills and you can find yourself wanting to eat despite the schedule you have set up. You have to constantly mentally repeat the mantra that you are stronger, the binge eating will not defeat you, you can wait a few more minutes, you can do it. Once you have mastered the art of keeping to your time-table, you are one step closer to achieving your aim.

The goal of setting up a time-table is to ensure a constant healthy eating pattern is put in place. You can arrange to have your three normal meals in a day and also incorporate some little healthy snacks just in between and before going to sleep at night too. This will help in breaking the circle of long periods of calorie restrictions and massive bingeing.

You always have to look out for number one: you. Take regular stock of the process and see how it is coming along for you. Make a few adjustments here and there if the need arises.

The food you binge on contains a lot of substances that elevates your mood very fast and also brings it down just as fast. They are mostly high in sugars which are quickly digested and the feelings of wanting more and hunger always set in very fast. Since most of the foods we consume have effects on our moods, you should focus more on food substances that will positively give you a good mood that is not temporary. Vegetables and fruits contains a lot of minerals and vitamins which are very effective in dealing with mood swings. The forms of sugars also to be taken should be highly complex because it takes a longer time for it to be digested and thus the calories are given to the body system at a reduced rate compared to simple sugars that give almost immediate highs and resultant lows with hunger pangs. Some good sources of such complex sugars are wheat, tubers, oatmeal, barley etc. Apart from the complex sugars or carbohydrates, you must ensure that you take in the major classes of food nutrients in the right proportions at the right time. Food substances rich in protein help in building the body system and defenses e.g. eggs, beans, meat, milk, etc.

In all of these as you plan and aim to execute your diet as best as you can, do not skip any of your snacks or meals no matter how inconvenient or stressful it may be. This will only open you wide to attacks from the binge. Arranging your meals ahead of time with foods you are comfortable with will mitigate this. When it is finally time for you to eat, make sure you eat slowly and savor every morsel. Do not rush it to prevent it from becoming a binge.

YOUR MEDICAL PRACTIONER

Due to the nature of the eating disorder having a dual component of mental and physical nature, there will come a point in your battle against binge eating when you may have to get medical assistant. Having a medical practitioner in your corner who will check and keep an eye on your treatment and recovery process is very important. He or she may also bring in further specialized help depending on the complexity of your condition. You do not have to be ashamed or anxious when you try opening up to your doctor though this is a common occurrence. Your problem is serious and you need all the help you can get so do not ever belittle your condition thinking you do not need any assistance when you cannot fight it all alone. Whatever your apprehensions are, take a bold step and communicate with your doctor. Most times, persons suffering from such conditions have a tough time speaking with a relative stranger. If you are in this group, then you can open up to someone who is well known to you like a family member or a friend who can give you candid advice. Such a person can then be your bridge to the doctor until such a time when you can comfortably relate with the doctor. You have to understand that your apprehension is a normal part of who you are at present and opening to someone who totally gets you is one step in the right direction towards attaining a good eating habit.

YOUR NUTRITIONIST

If you are trying to forge ahead with self-help, a nutritionist may be able to point you in the right direction for you to be able to fully understand the intricate connections between your mood, thoughts and the foods you eat. A nutritionist will help you set up a meal plan to strengthen your desire to fully recover will enjoying the eating process.

COUNSELLING AND PSYCHOTHERAPY

Your medical doctor after the initial examination may refer you for a counselling session or to a psychotherapist. This approach to treatment involves you talking about your fears and getting the proper advice from certified personnel. You discover emotions which have been buried deep within your subconscious and develop strategies of dealing with them. Every individual responds to this method differently and the length of time before appreciably results are obtained therefore varies. If yours is taking a bit longer to manifest, keep at it while exploring the proper mix of treatment methods that works best for your person.

FAMILY THERAPY

Your eating disorder does not just affect you only. It takes its toll on all your loved ones. Engaging in family therapy helps in seeking out ways of tackling the problem. This method is also used for a number of challenges that a family may be going through such as divorce or loss of loved ones. Your family members can help you in setting realistic targets. This form of therapy also helps everyone within the unit to study the working mechanisms of the family and how it may be giving power to your problem. Making positive changes to some of these kinks may in the long run be of great advantage to everyone.

YOUR FOOD DIARY

Putting into writing your eating habits is one very important way to monitor and change harmful eating practices. By making a record of the time, place and emotions which prompted you to eat, how you felt after eating, you are making a conscious step to changing your eating pattern. It is likely to be hard when starting this process and you may feel the urge to stop but you need to continue for you to be fully observant of what is happening just before you eat and the feelings experienced afterwards. Your diary should contain some of the following information; time you ate, nature of the food consumed, place where you ate, why did you actually eat at that particular time, was the food eaten due to normal hunger pangs or binge in response to a stimuli and the last one is how you felt just before and after eating.

Enter the records of your eating pattern regularly and study the data collected every other week to look out for patterns. Once you have observed both pros and cons, you can make adjustments to it to help you take charge of your eating habits. You must ensure that the information entered is as factual as possible if you are to be true to yourself. This can also be used with third parties who are specialists in the field of eating disorders who can help you analyze the data you have amassed to help you plan your diet and control the feelings associated with your bingeing disorder.

CHAPTER THREE

DEVELOPING LIFE SKILLS FOR HEALTHY EATING

What you are hoping to achieve involves a major overhaul of your current health state. This turn-around is not just centered on what you eat but on your life as a whole. This is not all about a perfect combination of foods, but about building your emotional and physical well-being in all spheres of life. You are in charge of what you eat so should decide on foods that you don't have to be compelled to eat but rather pick snacks and foods that you are familiar with and that will not lead to retrogression. Starting off, you are likely to focus on very low energy foods and this will pose no hindrances to your program as long as you take in healthy portions regularly. Focus on the fact that your eating is not about trying to take charge of your weight but on eating right to maintain a healthy lifestyle. By so doing, it will eventually dawn on you that eating what makes you feel good is what you will aim to have most times. Your food consumption if recorded conscientiously, you will be able to glean vital information from it indicating how to make appropriate changes to your unhealthy habit.

Having a well laid out strategy before every meal involves deciding on what to eat and how much to eat. Having an exit strategy which puts an end to the meal should also be in play. For example, a piece of cake or fruit can be your exit food. Once you have taken the pre-planned food, that is the end of that diet and practicing this for a couple of weeks becomes quite easy for you so that it becomes part of you and no conscious effort may be needed to carry it out later. Your plans should also include your shopping schedule and what you buy at any given time. Make sure you buy only what you absolutely need and do not buy too much trying to prepare for days you may be too busy to go shopping as this may prompt your bingeing with too much food all around you. Continue to record every move you make against this enemy and store the strategies that work best for you. You should take each battle at a time with your eyes on the ultimate goal of winning the war. You could have anything you want to eat at any time but it is pertinent that you keep to a regular routine to prevent you from eating out of just hunger.

Your diary will also give you a look into possible triggers. This will enable you to devise ways to limit such occurrences. The most probable reason for your bingeing may be due to having too much time on your hand with nothing keeping you busy. Most times it happens during festive periods when you are at home from school or break from work. To avoid this, ensure you plan ahead with activities to keep you busy during this period. Plan to meet up with friends and families or have them come over, go see movies, hiking, see a game of baseball or anything that makes you happy other than been all alone.

Have you ever had more than enough food than you actually need on your plate? It happens to a lot of us. In such a situation, learn to walk away and fight another day. Once you discover you are becoming satisfied with more food still remaining on your plate, you should develop the habit of stopping and probably storing the food for a later time or giving your dog or cat to feed on it. Do not at any time force yourself to finish everything you have on your plate if you are not up to it.

At the start of your program, you will notice your mind is totally filled up with thoughts of food. It can be quite hard pushing such thoughts away but you should know it is only natural and temporary. As you continue with your healing process, it becomes easier for you to plan your meals without dwelling too much on the thoughts of food throughout your day. At any point during your meal you have to be true to yourself. Do you still feel the urge to eat despite cleaning your plate of every morsel? You must not let the eating disorder control how much you take. Be in charge. Plan ahead on how much you will have at every meal and stick to that plan no matter the urge you feel before and immediately after each meal. This is possible by following your instinct of self-preservation to prevent the disorder from taking you down. If by peradventure you still remain hungry after your meals, stick to the current plan for a few more days and see how you feel. If your body finally adapts, then you continue with the meal plan. If not, then it is time to make changes to your program.

You also have to bring your loved ones into your plan from the onset as their knowledge and understanding of your condition will go a long way in supporting your change in diet habits. Inform them about what they should avoid around you like giving you foods or snacks to make you feel better. Your immediate family will also have to go through some changes. Have a meeting and explain in details what need to be done and ensure it is as flexible as can be. Do not impose your decision on them as this may be counter-productive in the end. Since you are adopting a new healthy eating habit, the whole family can really benefit from this too. So gently ease them into this new world.

PUT AN END TO DIETING

Your binge eating disorder is a complex interaction of several factors and totally understanding it can be quite hard. The binge eating disorder goes round in a cycle that is quite predictable and one major way to stop the vicious cycle is to put an end to dieting which is a major component in sustaining your eating disorder. The mere thought of stopping your dieting can send you into a panic as you may feel that the charge you have over your life may be lost resulting in another bingeing chapter. Accepting that your dieting fuels the cycle is one way of coming to terms with the health problems it is causing you and it will be much easier for you to stop dieting. Eating constantly at predetermined intervals instead of dieting will prevent you from adding more weight. Regular intake of calories will ensure that you shed some much needed body weight. It is common for your apprehension about your weight to stop you from stopping the dieting regime. To counter this, you can slowly ease out of it. Take a break for a while and check the outcome. Start with a regular eating plan and observe if there are positive changes by making regular input into your food diary.

LOOK OUT FOR NUMBER ONE

Your condition may have made you feel unhappy about your body leading to total neglect. You may feel a sense of disconnect from your body by not looking in the mirror or exposing your body to your partner or even at the beach. You can get back in tune with your body to enable you wear clothes you feel comfortable in, going to the spa, not putting out the light when getting in bed with your partner or going to the saloon for a new hairstyle. Engaging in physical activities can positively promote your new lifestyle. Your metabolic process is increased and the propensity to binge is greatly reduced. Get involved in some form of exercise that you enjoy wholesomely and that will not stress out your system unnecessarily. Too much pressure is to be avoided. There is no need to go all out just to be fit. You can do simple aerobics at home, walking or jogging around your neighborhood will suffice. Having a fixed time incorporated into your daily activities will go a long way. It is important that you have this time as at the time you have set for it. It is your time and don't let distractions set in. Rather, you can bring in your little distractions into you daily exercise so that there is a happy blend and no part of your life will suffer any significant neglect.

We as humans experience a wide range of emotions and accepting what we feel enables us to find ways of dealing with it. There are no clear cut ways to categorize what you feel at any point in time as it may be linked to certain external stimuli that you will respond to in various ways depending on your present state of mind. If put in a tight corner to deliver on a favor or task, you have the choice to refuse and simply walk away instead of getting angry or letting depression set in because of all the pressure. You first have to make yourself feel good and happy before looking out for anyone else. You should respond to situations in ways that puts you in charge and soothes your emotions.

It will not all be smooth sailing as there will be days with dark clouds overhead. You may just want to throw in the towel and go back to your old bad habits. You need to immediately take a step back and objectively look at the situation and develop plans on how to handle it. When such situations arise, you may not be able to handle it all by yourself so it can be of great help to you if you have a loved one or professional you can reach out to who will gently steer you back to the right path. When you feel things are not going according to plan, the most important thing you can do is to stick with your meal plan and try as much as possible not to deviate as it will immediately bring about your bingeing. If you did fall off the wagon, try as much as possible to not beat yourself over it. You have to continue to build a positive outlook as any setback you encounter is a learning curve that will build your self-will and esteem. You have to build on your past experiences and apply the methods you used in dealing with it to your current situation. Your goal here is to drastically cut down on the amount of times you fail and not setting up yourself not to ever fail again. It is just a minor setback and that is what it is. Have a positive mindset about the days you have been able to overcome the urge and look on to build on that.

CHAPTER FOUR

PUTTING AN END TO BINGEING

The binge cycle keeps you chained to thinking it will help you deal with feelings you have no control over. Your whole body system is now in tune with certain food types that gives you short-lived highs to make you relaxed. However, you need to make moves to try as much as possible to prevent you from bingeing again no matter how hard it may look to you now.

First you must try as much as possible to do things at the right time. Do not let all your duties pile up until you begin to be feel pressured which is not good for you. Arrange all your duties into a working schedule which will get done at the right time without delaying and eventually causing a back log. Who are you closest to and can open up to about what is bothering you at any given time? It is imperative that you have a network of people you can reach out to when you are in need. You need to know when to shut down and let some steam off. Find activities that soothe your nerves and calms you down. Engage in a few until you find what actually works for you. It may be watching a movie, reading a novel, taking a walk or a power nap. Why keep so much food around when you have no intention of actually eating it? They are a source of temptation and may lead you to binge in the not too distant future. If you are not yet strong enough to control your eating urges, then it is not advisable that you have foods that can trigger your compulsion around. Have just enough food that will last you for a few days and ensure that they are not sugary foods.

CHAPTER FIVE

HELPING YOUR FRIEND WITH A BINGE EATING DISORDER

Our friends and loved ones most times are under so much burden suffering from their eating disorders in secret. They are usually ashamed to let us know for fear about how we will react to it. At this stage in their lives, they need your support in this battle. Possibly when a friend opens up to you and you are out of your depths as to how to assist, talk your friend into getting professional help. Whenever you want to talk to your friend about something important, avoid meal times. Arrange a meeting at a place where the two of you can have a private talk. A large crowd or family may be too much for them to handle.

As you try to ensure you are available for your friend, you also need to find out more about his/her condition by getting more materials to educate yourself. You also need to be quite observant to some behavioral patterns your friend may be hiding that are pointers to the disorder. You should be very tactful when approaching your friend about your findings because some people do not like their privacy invaded in such a manner and they may feel you are trying to take away their coping mechanisms.

Do not engage in talks about weight and body image issues with them. Also avoid pestering them to eat more, exercise or to open up. It may cause your friend to clam up and move away from you. There is so much that you can do as a friend. So you need to give yourself some limits on how far you can go in helping your friend to prevent you from taking on the responsibility of catering for your friend. You should know that it is a long journey to recovery and can be very slow and painful.

WORDS OF ENCOURAGEMENT

As a binge eater, you need to have some positive affirmations that will strengthen your resolve to overcome the disorder. Write out some words of encouragement and put it where you can see it often around your home and in your office. Your condition is temporary and it will be gone real soon, you just need to be strong and continue eating healthy. Adore your body no matter your present size. Do not let yourself be guilt tripped about the so called "normal" body sizes. You are you and unique. No one can be you.

Love yourself totally and unabashedly. It is all about you before anyone else. So focus on you. You will not accuse anyone about your condition, you will take measures to ensure you eat normally again no matter how long it takes.

You need to let the real you come out and not this person you are now. Each day is a gift and live it not just to eat but to enjoy every breathing moment.

Hope you found this book helpful? You can contact me at Jason.B.Tiller@gmail.com for more one on one discussions. Thanks you.

Made in the USA
Las Vegas, NV
01 May 2021

22310521R00042